BOOKS BY PHILIP LEVINE

THE MERCY   1999
UNSELECTED POEMS   1997
THE SIMPLE TRUTH   1994
WHAT WORK IS   1991
NEW SELECTED POEMS   1991
A WALK WITH TOM JEFFERSON   1988
SWEET WILL   1985
SELECTED POEMS   1984
ONE FOR THE ROSE   1981
7 YEARS FROM SOMEWHERE   1979
ASHES: POEMS NEW AND OLD   1979
THE NAMES OF THE LOST   1976
1933   1974
THEY FEED THEY LION   1972
RED DUST   1971
PILI'S WALL   1971
NOT THIS PIG   1968
ON THE EDGE   1963

ESSAYS

THE BREAD OF TIME   1994

TRANSLATIONS

OFF THE MAP: SELECTED POEMS OF
GLORIA FUERTES, EDITED AND TRANSLATED
WITH ADA LONG   1984

TARUMBA: THE SELECTED POEMS OF
JAIME SABINES, EDITED AND TRANSLATED
WITH ERNESTO TREJO 1979

INTERVIEWS

DON'T ASK   1981

THE SIMPLE TRUTH

THE SIMPLE TRUTH

POEMS BY

PHILIP LEVINE

ALFRED A. KNOPF   NEW YORK   2002

www.randomhouse.com/knopf/poetry/

My thanks to the editors of the following publications in which these poems first appeared:
ATLANTIC: "Magpiety" *and* "Ode for Mrs. William Settle"
BOULEVARD: "Ask for Nothing"
COLORADO REVIEW: "Out by Dark" *and* "My Brother Abel, the Wounded"
THE FORWARD: "My Father with Cigarette Twelve Years before the Nazis Could Break his Heart"
GEORGIA REVIEW: "The Trade"
HUDSON REVIEW: "Getting There," "The Old Testament," "In the Dark," *and* "Blue and Blue"
THE NATION: "Dreaming in Swedish," "The Return," *and* "Winter Words, Manhattan" (under the title "Ask the Snow")
THE NEW YORKER: "On the Meeting of García Lorca and Hart Crane," "Lame Ducks, McKesson and Robbins, 1945," "February 14th," "The Escape," "The Simple Truth," "No Buyers," "My Sister's Voice," "The Spanish Lesson," "My Mother with Purse the Summer they Murdered the Spanish Poet," *and* "Dust and Memory"
PARIS REVIEW: "Edward Lieberman, Entrepreneur"
PLOUGHSHARES: "Blue"
POETRY: "Tristan," "Photography," *and* "One Day"
PRINCETON LIBRARY CHRONICLE: "Llanto"
THREEPENNY REVIEW: "Soul," "The Poem of Chalk," *and* "Listen Carefully"

Library of Congress Cataloging-in-Publication Data

Levine, Philip
The simple truth : poems / by Philip Levine.
    p.   cm.
    ISBN 0–679–76584–0
    I. Title.
PS3562.E9S56   1994   94-14508
811'.54—dc20   CIP

Manufactured in the United States of America
Published November 1, 1994
Reprinted Twice
Fourth Printing, October 2002

FOR MY BROTHERS,
WITH ME FROM THE START

CONTENTS

Contents

I

ON THE MEETING OF GARCIA LORCA AND HART CRANE

Brooklyn, 1929. Of course Crane's
been drinking and has no idea who
this curious Andalusian is, unable
even to speak the language of poetry.
The young man who brought them
together knows both Spanish and English,
but he has a headache from jumping
back and forth from one language
to another. For a moment's relief
he goes to the window to look
down on the East River, darkening
below as the early night comes on.
Something flashes across his sight,
a double vision of such horror
he has to slap both his hands across
his mouth to keep from screaming.
Let's not be frivolous, let's
not pretend the two poets gave
each other wisdom or love or
even a good time, let's not
invent a dialogue of such eloquence
that even the ants in your own
house won't forget it. The two
greatest poetic geniuses alive
meet, and what happens? A vision
comes to an ordinary man staring
at a filthy river. Have you ever
had a vision? Have you ever shaken
your head to pieces and jerked back
at the image of your young son
falling through open space, not
from the stern of a ship bound
from Vera Cruz to New York but from
the roof of the building he works on?
Have you risen from bed to pace
until dawn to beg a merciless God
to take these pictures away? Oh, yes,

let's bless the imagination. It gives
us the myths we live by. Let's bless
the visionary power of the human—
the only animal that's got it—,
bless the exact image of your father
dead and mine dead, bless the images
that stalk the corners of our sight
and will not let go. The young man
was my cousin, Arthur Lieberman,
then a language student at Columbia,
who told me all this before he died
quietly in his sleep in 1983
in a hotel in Perugia. A good man,
Arthur, he survived graduate school,
later came home to Detroit and sold
pianos right through the Depression.
He loaned my brother a used one
to compose his hideous songs on,
which Arthur thought were genius.
What an imagination Arthur had!

ODE FOR MRS. WILLIAM SETTLE

In Lake Forest, a suburb of Chicago,
a woman sits at her desk to write
me a letter. She holds a photograph
of me up to the light, one taken
17 years ago in a high school class
in Providence. She sighs, and the sigh
smells of mouth wash and tobacco.
If she were writing by candlelight
she would now be in the dark, for
a living flame would refuse to be fed
by such pure exhaustion. Actually
she is in the dark, for the man
she's about to address in her odd prose
had a life span of 125/th of a second
in the eye of a Nikon, and then he
politely asked the photographer to
get lost, whispering the request so as
not to offend the teacher presiding.
Those students are now in their thirties,
the Episcopal girls in their plaid skirts
and bright crested blazers have gone
unprepared, though French speaking, into
a world of liars, pimps, and brokers.
2.7% have died by their own hands,
and all the others have considered
the act at least once. Not one now
remembers my name, not one recalls
the reading I gave of Cesar Vallejo's
great *Memorium* to his brother Miguel,
not even the girl who sobbed and
had to be escorted to the school nurse,
calmed and sent home in a cab. Evenings
in Lake Forest in mid-December drop
suddenly; one moment the distant sky
is a great purple canvas, and then it's
gone, and no stars emerge, however
not the least hint of the stockyards

or slaughter houses is allowed to drift
out to the suburbs, so it's a deathless
darkness with no more perfume than
cellophane. "Our souls are mingling
now somewhere in the open spaces
between Illinois and you," she writes.
When I read the letter two weeks
later, forwarded by my publisher,
I will suddenly discover a truth
of our lives on earth, and I'll bless
Mrs. William Settle of Lake Forest
for giving me more than I gave
her, for addressing me as Mr. Levine,
the name my father bore, a name
a man could take with courage
and pride into the empire of death.
I'll read even unto the second page
unstartled by the phrase, "By now
you must have guessed, I am
a dancer." Soon snow will fall
on the Tudor houses of the suburbs
turning the elegant parked sedans
into anonymous mounds, the winds
will sweep in over the Rockies
and across the great freezing plains
where America first died, winds
so fierce boys and men turn their backs
to them and simply weep, and yet
in all that air the soul of Mrs. William
Settle will not release me, not even
for one second. Male and female,
aged and middle aged, we ride it out
blown eastward toward our origins,
one impure being become wind. Above
the Middle West, truth and beauty
are one though never meant to be.

LAME DUCKS,
MCKESSON & ROBBINS, 1945

Late Friday afternoon in the final year
of the Second World War, Stanley and I
gazed from the men's head on the fourth floor,

when downriver they came, a flotilla of ducks
breasting the waters of our river
headed toward the magic isles of Hamtramck.

We had shaved and patted our cheeks with cologne
stolen from "Sundries." We had washed
as heroes in movies do, standing before

an open window so that women might mark
the line from armpit to crotch scrubbed clean
to the roots of the sparse thatch going dark.

Redressed in our pressed white T-shirts we smoked
and sipped from a bottle of paregoric
stolen from "Addictive Medicines," and talked

of the whole weekend that spread out before us.
Down below, patched with light, the river rode on
toward the waiting darkness. And then the ducks

appeared, a little gliding V of seven,
perhaps a family, perhaps not. "Canadian
teals," said I. "No," said Stanley, "birds of heaven."

Their plumage caught the colors of the world,
their bills were gleaming and pliant, their black rumps
calm above the shadowy undercurrents as past

the Bob-Lo boat where it discharged its cargo
of daytime revellers they swept and past the moored
and serious boats to Buffalo and out

of sight to find a shore that they might waddle up
to settle down to nesting. But first the war
had to end in Asia, the river had to burn,

Stanley had to brush his teeth and comb his hair
seven times and fluff it up and grease it down.
I had to fall off a ladder to the stars

and break my right forearm and flunk calculus
so as predicted at my initial birth
I'd be good for nothing but to tell you this.

FEBRUARY 14TH

Awakening at dawn thirty-
six years ago, I see
the lifting of her eyelids
welcome me home. I can
recall her long arms en-
circling me, and I reach
out until the moment slides
into all the forgotten hours.
All the rest of our lives
the tree outside that window
groans in the wind. In other
rooms we'll hear other houses
mutter and won't care, and
go on hearing and not
caring until our names
merge with the wind. One
room, bare, uncurtained,
in a city long ago lost,
goes with us into the wide
measureless light. A tune
goes with us too. Hear
it in the little weirs
collecting winter waters,
in the drops of frozen rain
ticking from the eaves to
pool in the tiny valleys
of their making. Six weeks,
and the wide world is green

ONE DAY

Everyone knows that the trees will go one day
and nothing will take their place.
Everyone has wakened, alone, in
a room of fresh light and risen
to meet the morning as we did.
How long have we waited
quietly by the side of the road
for someone to slow and ask why.
The light is going, first from between
the long rows of dark firs
and then from our eyes, and when
it is gone we will be gone.
No one will be left to say,
"He took the stick and marked off
the place where the door would be,"
or "she held the child in both hands
and sang the same few tunes
over and over."
                    Before dinner we stood
in line to wash the grease from our faces
and scrub our hands with a hard brush,
and the pan of water thickened and grayed,
a white scum frothed on top,
and the last one flung it in the yard.
Boiled potatoes, buttered and salted, onions,
thick slices of bread, cold milk
almost blue under the fading light,
the smell of coffee from the kitchen.
I felt my eyes slowly closing.
You smoked in silence.
                    What life
were we expecting? Ships sailed
from distant harbors without us,
the telephone rang and no one answered,
someone came home alone and stood
for hours in the dark hallway.
A woman bowed to a candle

and spoke as though it could hear,
as though it could answer.
My aunt went to the back window
and called her small son, gone now
27 years into the closed wards
of the state, called his name again
and again. What could I do?
Answer for him who'd forgotten
his name? Take my father's shoes
and go into the streets?
                         Yes, the sun
has risen again. I can see the windows
change and hear a dog barking. The wind
buckles the slender top of the alder,
the conversation of night birds
hushes, and I can hear my heart
regular and strong. I will live to see
the day end as I lived to see
the earth turn molten and white,
then to metal, then to whatever shape
we stamped into it as we laughed
the long night hours away or sang
how the eagle flies on Friday.
When Friday came, the early hours perfect
and cold, we cursed our only lives
and passed the bottle back and forth.
                                Some died.
I turned and he was gone, my friend
with the great laugh who walked
cautiously and ate with his head
down, like a bear, his coarse hair
almost touching the plate. The tall one
with arms no thicker than a girl's,
who cursed his swollen face
as though he could have another.
The one whose voice lilted softly
when he raised a finger and spoke. I sat

beside him, trying to describe the sea
as I had seen it, but it was lost,
distant and unseen, perhaps no longer
there under a low sky. I tried to tell him
how the waves darkened and left only
the sound of their breaking,
and after a silence we learned to bear,
it all came back. He turned away
to the wall and slept, and I went out
into the city. It was I who'd held his wife
and felt the small bones of her back
rising and falling as she did not cry.
Later I would see my son from a distance
and not call out. I would waken that night
beside a sleeping woman and count
each breath.
                    Soon it was summer, afternoon,
the city hid indoors in the great heat,
the hot wind shrivelled our faces. I said,
"They're gone." The light turned from red
to green, and we went on. "If they're not here,"
you said, "where are they?" We both
looked into the sky as though
it were our only home. We drove on.
Nothing moved, nothing stirred
in the oven of this valley. What
was there left to say? The sky
was on fire, the air streamed
into the open windows. We broke free
beyond the car lots, the painted windows,
the all-night bars, the places
where the children gathered, and we just
went on and on, as far as we could
into a day that never ended.

ASK FOR NOTHING

Instead walk alone in the evening
heading out of town toward the fields
asleep under a darkening sky;
the dust risen from your steps transforms
itself into a golden rain fallen
earthward as a gift from no known god.
The plane trees along the canal bank,
the few valley poplars, hold their breath
as you cross the wooden bridge that leads
nowhere you haven't been, for this walk
repeats itself once or more a day.
That is why in the distance you see
beyond the first ridge of low hills
where nothing ever grows, men and women
astride mules, on horseback, some even
on foot, all the lost family you
never prayed to see, praying to see you,
chanting and singing to bring the moon
down into the last of the sunlight.
Behind you the windows of the town
blink on and off, the houses close down;
ahead the voices fade like music
over deep water, and then are gone;
even the sudden, tumbling finches
have fled into smoke, and the one road
whitened in moonlight leads everywhere.

SOUL

In Castelldefels we say, "There are four thousand souls
living in this village," not daring to omit even
the squat, gray haired captain of the *Guardia Civil*
or the trailer camp of Gypsies who thrive on a grassy plot
down by the tracks, the men who shine my wife's boots
while leering shamelessly up her skirt, the women
who beg at the tables of the open-air cantinas
in the public square, rolling their eyes and pinching
the borrowed babies until they bawl. As a child
I was embarrassed to implore the Lord to take my "soul,"
whatever that was, before I woke. I was five then,
living splendidly in a two-story house on the West Side
with fenced yard, heated garage, and a governess to tend
my brother and me, a Mrs. Morton, who professed
a faith in the afterlife and thought it charming
at bedtime to force the twin heathens to their knees
to recite her rhyming prayer, which we did only the once
as a circus act for company. Thankfully the Great Depression
saved us, and Mrs. Morton, caught pawning my mother's rings,
went packing—with no references—into the larger Christian world.
We moved, carless, to a dim, cramped walk-up behind
a used-car lot on Livernois. There my spiritual life
got a second start when I collapsed on the way to school
for no known reason and awakened staring up into the face
of a policeman with the improbable name of Officer German.
The school nurse, while fussing with my pulse and staring
at her watch, solemnly announced I must be dead,
and my mother was summoned from work to take me home
in a Checker cab. That night I lay face up on the couch
groping for words that might stay the inevitable.
I was allowed by the spirits that rule in such affairs
to return to life disguised as a seven-year old
not yet fully aware of the beauty of women's legs
or the firm skin that stretched across their gleaming sternums,
though Marta—our boarder from Nazi occupied Vienna—
asked me into her room one night to sample her talcums,
her colognes and creams, and to try on her silk garments,

which I stubbornly rejected, only to bring on a storm
of Middle Eastern abuse—a lost opportunity
I lived to regret. In the sixth grade, seated beside
a budding girl in pleated skirt and starched white blouse
I felt for the first time my present incarnation
taking hold, and though I fought it for days, though I begged
the unknown powers within me for relief, preferring
to remain rounded off and complete, the yin and yang
of the eleven-year old, it went on. Now the long torpors
could descend on me each spring. I became the object
and no longer the subject of my own sentence. When I asked
the inconstant stars that occasionally winked through
the dim air over Detroit for their guidance, they answered
in an indecipherable riot of words, Basque and Chinese,
which I alone could interpret. Thus the sudden flight
to Havana in 1947 in the hope of mastering
Latin ballroom dancing, my enlistment in the naval reserve
in order to acquire discipline and bearing, the marriage
to a fifteen-year old suburban delinquent. All of this failed,
just as the year on the night shift at Wonder Bread
and the diurnal sweats of the seven ovens failed
to rinse me of indignation. The surprise came when
on my twenty-sixth birthday while sober a grown woman
chose me, who was not sober, to father her children,
and together we embarked on a life we could call ours
in the village of Castelldefels in the year of our Lord
1965, where returning home alone on foot after a long day
of idling in the great cemetery of Barcelona, I shouted out
to the night sky, "There is that lot of me and all so luscious."
And believed it. I believe it now, even though
the squat captain of the *Guardia Civil* goes on censoring
my mail, the dwarf barber sneers as he calls me Don Felipe,
the butcher hints I lack the *cojones* to take her sister,
and each night the sea tears at the littered coast, the wind
rages through the pines, and—except for us—all four thousand
souls, some alone, some in pairs, huddle in their beds and pray.

THE TRADE

Crouching down in the loud morning air
of the docks of Genoa, with the gulls wheeling
overhead, the fishermen calling, I considered
for a moment, then traded a copy of T.S. Eliot
for a pocket knife and two perfect lemons.
The old man who engineered the deal held
the battered black *Selected Poems*, pushed
the book out at arm's length perusing the notes
to "The Wasteland" as though he understood them.
Perhaps he did. He sifted through the box
of lemons, sniffing the tough skins of several,
before finally settling on just that pair.
He worked the large blade back and forth
nodding all the while, and stopped abruptly
as though to say, Perfect! I had not
come all that way from America by way
of the Indies to rid myself of the burden
of a book that haunted me or even to say,
I've had it with middle age, poetry, my life.
I came only from Barcelona on the good ship
Kangaroo, sitting up on deck all night
with a company of conscript Spaniards
who passed around the black wine of Alicante
while they sang gypsy ballads and Sinatra.
We'd been six hours late getting started.
In the long May light the first beacons
along the Costa Brava came on, then France
slipped by, jewelled in the darkness, as I
dozed and drank by turns in the warm sea air
which calmed everything. A book my brother gave
twenty years before, out of love, stolen
from Doubleday's and brought to the hospital
as an offering, brother to brother, and carried
all those years until the words, memorized,
meant nothing. A grape knife, wooden handled,
fattened at one end like a dark fist, the blade
lethal and slightly rusted. Two lemons, one

for my pocket, one for my rucksack, perfuming
my clothes, my fingers, my money, my hair,
so that all the way to Rapallo on the train
I would stand among my second-class peers, tall,
angelic, an ordinary man become a gift.

LLANTO

for Ernesto Trejo

Plum, almond, cherry have come and gone,
the wisteria has vanished in
the dawn, the blackened roses rusting
along the barbed-wire fence explain

how April passed so quickly into
this hard wind that waited in the west.
Ahead is summer and the full sun
riding at ease above the stunned town

no longer yours. Brother, you are gone,
that which was earth gone back to earth,
that which was human scattered like rain
into the darkened wild eyes of herbs

that see it all, into the valley oak
that will not sing, that will not even talk.

IN THE DARK

In the last light of a summer day facing the Canadian shore
we watched from the island as night sifted into the river,
blackening the still surface. An ore boat passed soundlessly
trailing a tiny wake that folded in upon itself with a sigh,
unless that sigh was hers or mine. In the darkness it's hard
to tell who is listening and who is speaking. St. Augustine
claimed we made love in the dark— though he did not write
"made love"— because we were ashamed to do it in the sight
of anything, although I suppose God could see in the dark, having
at least as good eyesight as a cat. Our cat Nellie used to like
to watch my wife and me at love, but she was not a creature
who generalized and of all things she liked best a happy household.
"God loves a happy giver," I read in the Abyssinian chapel
on top of the Holy Sepulcher, which suggests the old saint
had no idea what he was talking about, but in the darkness
it's not easy to tell who is talking and who listening, who giving,
who taking, who praying, who cursing. Even then, watching
from the island, I thought that making love was a form of prayer.
You got down on your knees, if you were a boy, and prepared
        yourself
for whatever the future held in store, and no matter how firm
your plans without the power of another power you were lost.
It's so dark back then I can't tell what I'm thinking, although
I haven't placed my hand on Millie's shoulder for nothing,
nor have I turned my face toward Millie's merely to catch
a reflection of the darkness in her wide, hazel eyes, cat eyes
I called them then. Millie sighs, the ore boat passes silently
to disappear into a future that's still mysterious, I take a breath,
the deepest breath of my life, and knowing the generations of stars
are watching from above, I go down on my knees in prayer.

MAGPIETY

You pull over to the shoulder
    of the two-lane
road and sit for a moment wondering
    where you were going
in such a hurry. The valley is burned
    out, the oaks
dream day and night of rain
    which never comes.
At noon or just before noon
    the short shadows
are gray and hold what little
    life survives.
In the still heat the engine
    clicks, although
the real heat is hours ahead.
    You get out and step
cautiously over a low wire
    fence and begin
the climb up the yellowed hill.
    A hundred feet
ahead the trunks of two
    fallen oaks
rust; something passes over
    them, a lizard
perhaps or a trick of sight.
    The next tree
you pass is unfamiliar,
    the trunk dark,
as black as an olive's; the low
    branches stab
out, gnarled and dull: a carob
    or a Joshua tree.
A sudden flaring up ahead,
    a black-winged
bird rises from nowhere,
    white patches
underneath its wings, and is gone.

You hear your own
breath catching in your ears,
        a roaring, a sea
sound that goes on and on
        until you lean
forward to place both hands
        —fingers spread—
into the bleached grasses
        and let your knees
slowly down. Your breath slows
        and you know
you're back in central
        California
on your way to San Francisco
        or the coastal towns
with their damp sea breezes
        you haven't
even a hint of. But first
        you must cross
the Pacheco Pass. People
        expect you, and yet
you remain, still leaning forward
        into the grasses
that if you could hear them
        would tell you
all you need to know about
        the life ahead.

Out of a sense of modesty
        or to avoid the truth
I've been writing in the second
        person, but in truth
it was I, not you, who pulled
        the green Ford
over to the side of the road
        and decided to get
up that last hill to look

back at the valley
he'd come to call home.
　　I can't believe
that man, only thirty-two,
　　less than half
my age, could be the person
　　fashioning these lines.
That was late July of '60.
　　I had heard
all about magpies, how they
　　snooped and meddled
in the affairs of others, not
　　birds so much
as people. If you dared
　　to remove a wedding
ring as you washed away
　　the stickiness of love
or the cherished odors of another
　　man or woman,
as you turned away
　　from the mirror
having admired your newfound
　　potency—humming
"My Funny Valentine" or
　　"Body and Soul"—
to reach for a rough towel
　　or some garment
on which to dry yourself,
　　he would enter
the open window behind you
　　that gave gratefully
onto the fields and the roads
　　bathed in dawn—
he, the magpie—and snatch
　　up the ring
in his hard beak and shoulder
　　his way back

into the currents of the world
    on his way
to the only person who could
    change your life:
a king or a bride or an old woman
    asleep on her porch.

Can you believe the bird
    stood beside you
just long enough, though far
    smaller than you
but fearless in a way
    a man or woman
never could be? An apparition
    with two dark
and urgent eyes and motions
    so quick and precise
they were barely motions at all?
    When he was gone
you turned, alarmed by the rustling
    of oily feathers
and the curious pungency
    and were sure
you'd heard him say the words
    that could explain
the meaning of blond grasses
    burning on a hillside
beneath the hands of a man
    in the middle of
his life caught in the posture
    of prayer. I'd
heard that a magpie could talk,
    so I waited
for the words, knowing without
    the least doubt
what he'd do, for up ahead
    an old woman

waited on her wide front porch.
My children
behind her house played
in a silted pond
poking sticks at the slow
carp that flashed
in the fallen sunlight. You
are thirty-two
only once in your life, and though
July comes
too quickly, you pray for
the overbearing
heat to pass. It does, and
the year turns
before it holds still for
even a moment.
Beyond the last carob
or Joshua tree
the magpie flashes his sudden
wings, a second
flames and vanishes into the pale
blue air.
July 23, 1960.
I lean down
closer to hear the burned grasses
whisper all I
need to know. The words rise
around me, separate
and finite. A yellow dust
rises and stops
caught in the noon's driving light.
Three ants pass
across the back of my reddened
right hand.
Everything is speaking or singing.
We're still here.

II

THE POEM OF CHALK

On the way to lower Broadway
this morning I faced a tall man
speaking to a piece of chalk
held in his right hand. The left
was open, and it kept the beat,
for his speech had a rhythm,
was a chant or dance, perhaps
even a poem in French, for he
was from Senegal and spoke French
so slowly and precisely that I
could understand as though
hurled back fifty years to my
high school classroom. A slender man,
elegant in his manner, neatly dressed
in the remnants of two blue suits,
his tie fixed squarely, his white shirt
spotless though unironed. He knew
the whole history of chalk, not only
of this particular piece, but also
the chalk with which I wrote
my name the day they welcomed
me back to school after the death
of my father. He knew feldspar,
he knew calcium, oyster shells, he
knew what creatures had given
their spines to become the dust time
pressed into these perfect cones,
he knew the sadness of classrooms
in December when the light fails
early and the words on the blackboard
abandon their grammar and sense
and then even their shapes so that
each letter points in every direction
at once and means nothing at all.
At first I thought his short beard
was frosted with chalk; as we stood
face to face, no more than a foot

apart, I saw the hairs were white,
for though youthful in his gestures
he was, like me, an aging man, though
far nobler in appearance with his high
carved cheekbones, his broad shoulders,
and clear dark eyes. He had the bearing
of a king of lower Broadway, someone
out of the mind of Shakespeare or
García Lorca, someone for whom loss
had sweetened into charity. We stood
for that one long minute, the two
of us sharing the final poem of chalk
while the great city raged around
us, and then the poem ended, as all
poems do, and his left hand dropped
to his side abruptly and he handed
me the piece of chalk. I bowed,
knowing how large a gift this was
and wrote my thanks on the air
where it might be heard forever
below the sea shell's stiffening cry.

DREAMING IN SWEDISH

The snow is falling on the tall pale reeds
near the seashore, and even though in places
the sky is heavy and dark, a pale sun
peeps through casting its yellow light
across the face of the waves coming in.
Someone has left a bicycle leaning
against the trunk of a sapling and gone
into the woods. The tracks of a man
disappear among the heavy pines and oaks,
a large-footed, slow man dragging
his right foot at an odd angle
as he makes for the one white cottage
that sends its plume of smoke skyward.
He must be the mailman. A canvas bag,
half-closed, sits upright in a wooden box
over the front wheel. The discrete
crystals of snow seep in one at a time
blurring the address of a single letter,
the one I wrote in California and mailed
though I knew it would never arrive on time.
What does this seashore near Malmö
have to do with us, and the white cottage
sealed up against the wind, and the snow
coming down all day without purpose
or need? There is our canvas sack of answers,
if only we could fit the letters to each other.

OUT BY DARK

If you take the two-lane highway from Tetuan to Fez
you'll come to a crossroad near the halfway mark
where the signs are in Arabic and the numbers
have disappeared. If a man with a shepherd's crook
squats under a cedar tree and spits out the shells
of sunflower seeds, you've come to the right place.
Go down on your knees until you feel the cold rising
slowly through your thighs to settle in your hips.
The sunlight burns along the nape of your neck
urging your head downward and forward until you've
assumed the posture of prayer. It's an hour past noon
early in the year, and already the shadows darken
in the yellow grass and fill the canyons carved
by truck tires. You're too tired. You drove
all night through the sleeping Roman towns, Tarragona,
Alicante, the white village of Lorca, where the bread
tasted of nickel and phosphate. You slept outside
a cave with painted eyes and spoke only to yourself,
you crossed the straits, your face into the wind;
the salt water filling your ears like so much music
beaten out on a wet rock. The truth is you don't
want the truth at all. Listen at last in silence
to someone who is not wise, to someone
more lost than you: Under a leaking, pewter sky
in the mountain town of Moulay Idriss, I stopped
a tall stranger robed in the ragged cloak Esau
fled God in and asked where I might buy a bottle
of rain water or red wine. He nodded slowly.
"This is a holy city," he said. We stood face to face
on the single mud street that vanished ahead among
seven brown earthen shacks, each with a door closed
on the screeching of black birds. "So?" I said.
"So," he said in perfect English, "If you're not
out of here by dark I'll cut your throat," and he
smiled as he drew the wound across the small space
that separated us. So, I hitched a ride to Ceuta
with a German couple who dealt in rare pollens

that singed my nostrils. Near the parched beaches
of the Passaic I took up electronics and made my peace
with obsolescence. If you can't hear me at least
listen to the earth's prayer that gives off the perfume
of birth and worms or the psalms of dark wet wings.
Those are the magpies. They're settling around you
pretending there are grains of wheat in the pig grass,
seeds in the weed thick mounds, pretending they came
of their own accord or because they were curious,
pretending the rain keeps its promises. By half-past
seven tonight the world you lost will be one darkness,
a feather of velvet closed down, an eyelid of magpie.

THE RETURN: ORIHUELA, 1965

for Miguel Hernandez

You come over a slight rise
in the narrow, winding road
and the white village broods
in the valley below. A breeze
silvers the cold leaves
of the olives, just as you knew
it would or as you saw
it in dreams. How many days
have you waited for this day?
Soon you must face a son grown
to manhood, a wife to old age,
the tiny sealed house of memory.
A lone crow drops into the sun,
the fields whisper their courage.

GETTING THERE

Early August, hours west of Omaha,
I'd pulled to the side of the road to see
why the car was wobbling and sadly found
a front wheel had sheared off four bolts.
We were out of luck again. Early afternoon,
my youngest son and I hundreds of miles
from the house we'd left and the house
we aimed to find. The big rigs booming
by one after another, shaking the car
loaded with all we had, and the pale sky
riding above, cloudless and distant.
My heart pounded out of some need
to be heard, to address the land
without end, to strike a single chord
that would go on and on the way light
goes on and on seeking the last darkness
or that day went on in western Nebraska
forever in blinding sunlight or until
an old man in a Pontiac four-door stopped
to ask, Was we in trouble? and took us home
where he served buttermilk and crackers
while he phoned up the Ford people
they should see to it fast.
                                    You know how
a six year old blond, small for his age,
with a solemn, pensive air can almost
make your breath catch, your eyes fill
with tears, especially at those times
he will not explain the hidden sources
of his understanding. Such boys ask
for nothing. They simply stand in the center
of so large a place, quiet, accepting.
The old man took his hand as he walked
us around the borders of his farm, claiming
his ancient rights that sooner or later
the bank would claim. Acres of wheat,
a small garden where the onions were done,

gone to white seeds, the sweet corn
above our heads and rising. Three kinds
of tomatoes, sweet and chili peppers,
kept him busy. Handed up, my boy sat
grimly on the tractor seat holding fast
to the steering wheel as though the world
in its turning might buck him off,
his face fixed and serious. The old man
returned from the barn leading a goat
on a rope, a white goat named Ahab
as though he'd gotten the story wrong.
Teddy stared out over the acres of wheat
stretching all the way to those mountains
we had yet to cross, stared, and would not
begin to smile or come down to earth,
while the great day went on.
                           To be lost
in the center of America, to be taken in
by a stranger whose needs go unannounced,
to sleep beside your father, what can
it mean at six? He would grow to manhood,
leave home, risk the continent again
in far worse cars. Perhaps the lesson
never took or was no lesson but something else
about the open, wide gaze of a day
under the August sun, the gift of light
bronzing the wheat, the vast chord of sky
rolling across the fields, which answer
with their pips and squeaks. A second day
wakened downstairs with our host
stumbling into chairs, pipes groaning,
the one shrill note of coffee boiling
into bitterness. Perhaps the son saw
his father laugh this day, heard him
clink cups with the old man, and each
pour from the little screw-top bottle
to make it royal. After that old Aaron

drove us back to the highway, and we
stood beside the Ford miraculously
repaired and exchanged money and addresses
—for a small miracle has its price.
Now Aaron leans down to the window
to point the way ahead. He calls it west,
he mentions Colorado, the high mountains
snow-capped even now, and says nothing
about music, though the notes are rising
all around us, bird calls, exhaust roars,
the slap-slap of tires, the unheard cries
forming a new song, unheard, that wants
to be sung and won't. Holding up the map
for us, my son points out the roads
inked across the cracked and folded paper.
"Navigator," Aaron says, and Teddy smiles
at last, and now the three of us are laughing
at once, without harmony or reason.

BLUE

Dawn. I was just walking
back across the tracks
toward the loading docks
when I saw a kid climb
out of a boxcar, his blue
jacket trailing like a skirt,
and make for the fence. He'd
hoisted a wet wooden flat
of fresh fish on his right
shoulder, and he tottered
back and forth like someone
with one leg shorter than
the other. I took my glasses
off and wiped them on the tails
of my dirty shirt, and all
I could see were the smudges
of the men wakening one
at a time and reaching for
both the sky and the earth.
My brother-in-law, Joseph,
the railroad cop, who talked
all day and all night of beer
and pussy, Joseph in his suit
shouting out my name, Pheeel!
Pheeel! waving a blue bandana
and pointing behind me to
where the kid cleared the fence
and the weak March sun
had topped the car barns,
to a pale, watery sky, wisps
of dirty smoke, and the day.

BLUE AND BLUE

In mid-June the light hangs on until I think
the day will never end. At the table, alone,
I place my left hand, palm up, before me
and begin to count the little dry river beds
on the map of life. One means I will live
until I won't, another means someone else,
a third means children, a fourth the future's past,
and taken together they mean nothing at all.
I lose the count and turn the hand over to find
four blue streams with nowhere to go. In 1965
in late summer in the harbor of Barcelona
as I went out to sea, I did not know all
this hand could tell me. Overhead the sky darkened
into a blue so deep I thought the world would
break into fire. The evening wind swept from left
to right across the bow, and the waves broke
into blue, and in the deep trough of each wave
ran a current of richer blue. At that moment
I told myself I was not alone, I told myself
the meaning of everything was held in a single drop
of sea water the way all time crowded that moment.
I understood how one human being was everyone.
I must have said it aloud in English, for the man
next to me, a salesman from Argentina, turned
to ask my meaning. The sea was blue and beautiful,
was all I had the courage to say in his language.
He nodded slowly, and a dampened lock of white hair
fell across his brow. Men like that, with eyes
so crimped in wrinkles they can't possibly see out,
know everything. Or at least this one knew a fool
when he heard one, for he shoved his left hand
deeper into his jacket pocket and threw his cigar
into the face of the wind, where for a moment
it became so many meaningless dying fires.
Where was I going? you want to know. To sea.
The way young men in stories go to sea? No.
I worked for an American parts manufacturer

with headquarters in Chicago, I was nearly thirty-eight,
with a wife and three kids back in California.
I shared a state room on the good ship Kangaroo
bound for Genoa, where I meant to flog bearings,
drive shafts, and universal joints to merchants
far shrewder than I. Actually none of this matters.
When you were just nineteen you waited all summer
in Havana for a man to offer you a job
running guns into Bolivia, and that was how
you made your fortune, found the meaning of life,
and disappeared into cinema. Thus, it's not you
but I who must ask why the sea eats so many fires
or how a drop of salt water contains each moment.
It's hopeless. No one else wonders how each of us
became the other, no one else sits here asking
his own left hand what it holds, while outside
the mourning doves gather in the tall blond grass
under a sky that quickens into blue and blue.

TRISTAN

In all sorts of weather Tristan
would go out in the rowboat. As a child
I'd beg to go with him, but mother
would threaten me. Either I shut up
or she would take her stick to me,
and seeing how red her brow became,
how the veins in her neck thickened,
I would quiet. With the rain blowing
in from the sea, the front windows awash
with it, and the elms behind the house
wailing, I sometimes thought I
was at sea. I'd waken in the night
gone suddenly still and wonder if Tristan
was home in his little shed asleep
or pacing back and forth, bobbing up
and down on his short right leg.
From all these voyages he brought
back nothing of value, though once
he gave me a sea shell he said was
magic and had the secret knowledge
to predict the weather if listened to.
He took my hand in his cracked hand,
lifting it slowly to my ear and said,
"Hear." The wind caught in the elms
shouted a word, a name, I thought as
likely mine as any name, but all
I answered was, "Yes." Near the end
he brought back a thick green round
of glass the sea had polished and shaped
to a smooth stone. He pushed aside
his cup of coffee and his breakfast
slice of bread—it was early June,
the days long and warm, the sea at rest—
to place the glass, duller side up,
flat on my palm. "If ever you're lost
stare into this and you'll see the way."
Mother hollered at me, I grabbed up

my books and was off to school, laughing
to myself, for I could feel the glass,
cool and dark, hidden in my shirt pocket
where Tristan had slipped it. Before
the long windless days of August passed
his boat, nameless, but with one
brown staring eye painted on the bow
was sighted turning slowly in circles,
oarless, a mile from shore and towed
to its dock where it sat, idle,
until father had it hauled home on
the back of a flat bed truck and dropped
down in the garden, a creature of ocean
abruptly come to rest. Seasons passed,
autumn turned to winter and winter slowly
to spring. The bright blue paint flaked
off on the dirt, and then the one eye faded
to a woody gray and finally no eye at all.
One day I came back from school to find
the little boat filled to the brim
with fresh black dirt. Small green shoots
sprouted here and there where mother
had tamped them down by hand: thyme,
mint, sorrel, and some small flowers,
violets and impatiens that bloomed
before the summer ended. Nameless,
the boat sinks deeper into the earth
each year, though to myself I call
it Tristan and hear in the ragged
howling of the elms at night the name
come back to me again and again.
I carry the name with me, secretly,
saying it over and over as a charm,
for like the green glass round,
scarred now, and hidden in my wallet
at all times, it urges me out to sea.

DUST AND MEMORY

A small unshaven man, perhaps fifty,
with a peaked cap pulled sideways
to hide his features. He bowed his head
to the ground, groaned, rose to thrust
his head back in abandon, and flung
his body forward again. A supplicant
on his knees to what? The earth and sea
that had misused him? The power of pain?
The female God-face painted on the prow
of the fishing boat whose shade he hid in?
When the cap fell away I recognized a man
I passed each evening coming home at dusk,
a near neighbor to whom I'd never spoken
and never would. After dark I did not
steal back to find him gone or to hear
the sea, moonless, itself only a word
without consonants, repeated invisibly
inside my head.
                    What is this about?
Wherever you are now there is earth
somewhere beneath you waiting to take
the little you leave. This morning I rose
before dawn, dressed in the cold, washed
my face, ran a comb through my hair
and felt my skull underneath, unrelenting,
soon the home of nothing. The wind
that swirled the sand that day years ago
had a name that will outlast mine
by a thousand years, though made of air,
which is what I too shall become, hope-
fully, air that says quietly in your ear,
"I'm dust and memory, your two neighbors
on this cold star." That wind, the *Levante*,
will howl through the sockets of my skull
to make a peculiar music. When you hear it,
remember it's me, singing, gone but here,
warm still in the fire of your care.

THE ESCAPE

To come to life in Detroit is to be manufactured
without the power of speech. You clasp hands,
as I did, with a brother and step by step
begin the slow descent into hell or Hamtramck
and arrive, designed, numbered, tagged.
It was the year Hoover took office. Since then
I've been recycled seven times and escaped
myself twice. The second time I ran my hand
down the body next to me and felt my callused hand
touching *me*. She and I hushed in a room
I rented for $12 a month down the street
from the shabby little zoo. How late I came
to love, 26 years old, and for the first time
I became a woman, a singular woman who loved me
more than I loved myself. What had I been?
What do you think? Isn't it obvious? I was a child.
And then I discovered Luckys, and then I suppose
I created out of lies, bad teeth, and so much meat,
bone, and hair a character in the shape of a man.
Then I registered for the draft and it was official.
Case closed, 1A, classified to die before I came of age
unless Hiroshima and Nagasaki burned. They did,
and I celebrated by drinking myself into a stupor
that lasted eight years.
                              The first time I escaped
I'd gone out after dinner and the dishes were done
to be alone. In the dark I found the tree,
a copper beech, and climbed into the crotch
and leaned back against a heavy branch and let
the stars pass slowly above. At first cars
groaned one at a time on the Outer Drive,
then they did not, and besides the wind stirring
the hard black leaves there was only the roar
of my mind touching itself carefully with rain,
the first few drops filling my eyes, that day's
rain falling hours later from the leaves above,
wind shaken, and then the odor of earth rising

like the breath of a strange God I could love.
Can you imagine inhaling God at age fourteen
with lungs still untainted by cigarettes?
Little wonder I fell out of the tree and sprawled
face down, unhurt, my fingers spread wide
as though to take handfuls of last year's
brittle leaves into my mouth. Hours later
I rose in the shape of a boy named Phil,
but now myself.
               I'm an American,
even before I was fourteen I knew I would have
to create myself. My beautiful literature teacher,
Miss Hardman, who wore gloves on summer days,
who had a secret love for me she could
barely contain, had whispered this one day
as we passed in the hall and fought to still
the urge to take my head in her ungloved hands
and press my soul into her breasts. If she
had not nursed that unacted desire
I might have discovered love before
I was ready and lost it, never to awaken
in a rented room thirteen years later
transformed into an angel gifted with both
sexes and no wings. Because we were Midwestern
someone always had to pay: Johnny Moradian
had to be blown apart on Okinawa, Silas Nance
had to despise himself before my eyes, weeping
and weeping because a woman belittled him,
Jewel Sprague had to run off to Peru and disappear
in the Andes, my tiny French cousin had to walk
by night from Nîmes to the hills freezing
above Florence to survive the Nazis and succumb
to his own heart, my lost uncle had to stab
a man to death behind a bar on First Avenue
and beg God to punish him. Oh Lord of Life,
how much you made them pay so I could love.

THE SIMPLE TRUTH

I bought a dollar and a half's worth of small red potatoes,
took them home, boiled them in their jackets
and ate them for dinner with a little butter and salt.
Then I walked through the dried fields
on the edge of town. In middle June the light
hung on in the dark furrows at my feet,
and in the mountain oaks overhead the birds
were gathering for the night, the jays and mockers
squawking back and forth, the finches still darting
into the dusty light. The woman who sold me
the potatoes was from Poland; she was someone
out of my childhood in a pink spangled sweater and sunglasses
praising the perfection of all her fruits and vegetables
at the road-side stand and urging me to taste
even the pale, raw sweet corn trucked all the way,
she swore, from New Jersey. "Eat, eat," she said,
"Even if you don't I'll say you did."
                              Some things
you know all your life. They are so simple and true
they must be said without elegance, meter and rhyme,
they must be laid on the table beside the salt shaker,
the glass of water, the absence of light gathering
in the shadows of picture frames, they must be
naked and alone, they must stand for themselves.
My friend Henri and I arrived at this together in 1965
before I went away, before he began to kill himself,
and the two of us to betray our love. Can you taste
what I'm saying? It is onions or potatoes, a pinch
of simple salt, the wealth of melting butter, it is obvious,
it stays in the back of your throat like a truth
you never uttered because the time was always wrong,
it stays there for the rest of your life, unspoken,
made of that dirt we call earth, the metal we call salt,
in a form we have no words for, and you live on it.

III

NO BUYERS

Two books in Spanish
on the children of
the clouds, an electric
motor for a fan and no
fan blade, three spotted
eggs, uncracked. Bend
down and look: the eggs
are almost new. They glow
like the just born or
the just dead, feel
the heat as it passes
through your hand. Three
perfect shapes a thousand
sciences could not
improve, for sale to
anyone. A light snow
drifts down, perhaps
it's only shards of
paper, falling from
city hall, perhaps it's
light in tiny diamonds
meant to consecrate
the day or dirty it.
The keepers of this
shop—can we call them
shopkeepers, though in
the filthy air there's
nothing here to keep
except their distance
and their stillness?—
are river people. You
can tell by the way
the lines swirl away
from their eyes and race
off in all directions,
you can tell by the way
the man squats and does

not spit. Underneath,
the BMT rumbles on its
way to an ocean these two
will never see again.
The street rocks; the man
and woman hold. Garter
and panty set bunched against
the cold, the black broken
teeth of an old comb,
a plastic, satin-lined
casket for fountain pens,
a dusting of snow or more
tired paper. All these
riches set out on a blanket
from Samarkand or Toledo
that bears in black
the outline of the great
bird beneath whose wings
we flew out of the fires
of morning. A bus hisses
past for the seventh time,
sighing. A cop stops and
talks to no one, and he
sighs too. The clouds go
on clawing overhead. Children
rise from the underground
or descend in streams from
the clouds. For a moment
there is music and then not.
Light drains from above and
runs like melted lead into
the open steaming vents.
Side by side these two stand
while the day passes or
an hour passes in the almost
new dark as the three eggs
hatch into smaller and newer
eggs and nobody buys.

WINTER WORDS, MANHATTAN

When the young farm laborer
steals the roses for his wife
we know for certain he'll find
her beyond their aroma
or softness. We can almost
feel with how soft a step
he approaches the cottage
there on the edge of the forest
darkening even before supper,
not wanting to give away
the surprise, which shall be his
only, for now she sleeps beyond
surprise in the long full,
dreamless sleep he will soon
pray for. And so they become
a bouquet for a grave, a touch
of rose in a gray and white
landscape. All this years ago
in the imagination of a poet
who would die before the book
was published. Did the thorns
puncture the young man's fingers
as he pressed the short stems
through the knife blade? Did he
bleed on the snow like a man
in a film, on the tight buds,
on her face as he bent down
to take her breath? Did that
breath still smell of breakfast,
of raw milk and bread? What does
breath that doesn't come smell of,
if it smells at all? If I went
to the window now and gazed
down at the city stretching
in clear winter sunlight past
the ruined park the children
never visit, out over the rooftops

of Harlem past the great bridge
to Jersey and the country lost
to me before I found it,
would I cry and for whom?

MY SISTER'S VOICE

Half asleep in my chair, I hear
a voice quiver the windowpane,
the same high cry of fear I first
heard beside the Guadalquivir
when I wakened to wind and rain
and called out to someone not there
and heard an answer. That was Spain
twenty-six years ago. The voice hers,
my sister's, and now it's come again
to ask how we go on without her.
That night beside the great river
I dressed in the dark and alone
left my family and walked till dawn
came, freezing, on the eastern rim
of mountains. I found no answer,
or learned never to ask, for
the wind answers itself if you
wait long enough. It turns one way,
then another, the trees bend, they
rise, the long grasses wave and bow,
all the voices you've ever heard
you hear again until you know
you've heard nothing. And so I wait
motionless, and as the air calms
my small, lost sister grows quiet,
as shy as she was in her life.
I remember coming back that night
in Sevilla past the rail yards,
trying to hold on to each word
she'd spoken even as the words fled
from my mouth. The switch engines
steamed in the cold. The sentry
in a brown cap sat up to shake
himself awake, and with no fire,
no human cry and no bird song,
the day broke over everything.

THE OLD TESTAMENT

My twin brother swears that at age thirteen
I'd take on anyone who called me kike
no matter how old or how big he was.
I only wish I'd been that tiny kid
who fought back through his tears, swearing
he would not go quietly. I go quietly
packing bark chips and loam into the rose beds,
while in his memory I remain the constant child
daring him to wrest Detroit from lean gentiles
in LaSalle convertibles and golf clothes
who step slowly into the world we have tainted,
and have their revenge. I remember none of this.
He insists, he names the drug store where I poured
a milkshake over the head of an Episcopalian
with quick fists as tight as croquet balls.
He remembers his license plate, his thin lips,
the exact angle at which this seventeen year old dropped
his shoulder to throw the last punch. He's making
it up. Wasn't I always terrified?
"Of course," he tells me, "that's the miracle,
you were even more scared than me, so scared
you went insane, you became a whirlwind,
an avenging angel."
                        I remember planting
my first Victory Garden behind the house, hauling
dark loam in a borrowed wagon, and putting in
carrots, corn that never grew, radishes that did.
I remember saving for weeks to buy a tea rose,
a little stick packed in dirt and burlap,
my mother's favorite. I remember the white bud
of my first peony that one morning burst
beside the mock orange that cost me 69¢.
(Fifty years later the orange is still there,
the only thing left beside a cage for watch dogs,
empty now, in what had become a tiny yard.)
I remember putting myself to sleep dreaming
of the tomatoes coming into fullness, the pansies

laughing in the spring winds, the magical wisteria
climbing along the garage, and dreaming of Hitler,
of firing a single shot from a foot away, one
that would tear his face into a caricature of mine,
tear stained, bloodied, begging for a moment's peace.

PHOTOGRAPHY

My aunt Yetta sleeps, her mouth hanging open, her eyes
buried under a swirl of dark hair. When I rise
from bed I find her clothes scattered across
the flowered carpet. It's Sunday, a boy's voice
calls to me from the yard below, the voice of Harold Lux
impatient for play, urging me out into the city
we think is ours. From up here the elms glisten
in last night's rain, the still pools on the pavement
give back a cloudless sky going gray. A single car
starts up next door, dies, starts again. The toolmaker
leaves for work shaking his head as though his hair
were a mop of fire. In her wool bathrobe his wife
stands on the lawn in cotton socks, one hand clutching
a hankie, the other waving at the empty street.
Then what? November darkness and the cold wind,
the first snow bowing the bare branches; that wind
dies into streams of melting ice racing toward the river.
Black walnut, elm, great spreading copper beech,
maple greening into leaf, the bare lots flowering,
morning after morning a perfect sky until I think
I see heaven waiting at the end of the block. I turn
back to Aunt Yetta. The clock says more than heaven.
I have searched through cartons of old pictures
for what remained of that day, for even the moment
after the street went quiet. I have gone for years
with one hand held out before me as a token
of my blindness. Smeared by a thumb print, Yetta
broods in bright sunlight off to one side while
the others lean forward, ignorant and laughing,
into a future that is fixed. The lake behind them
changed its name. Today it's no more than a pond
I walk around each autumn looking for messages
among the fallen acorns and the beer cans
left by teenagers. Another engine fires, the air
rings with each precise explosion, and each image
vanishes into photography. When the children called
from the back seat, "Are we there yet? Are we there?"

what could we answer? We said the little we knew:
"We're still here." If you asked if Harold stands now
out in the decaying yard, faithful to the end,
breathing a name into the October air, what
could I do but shake my head and go dumb? Perhaps
it's enough to say what I can. The toolmaker
wore his only suit, the light blue one, for days
after his wife ran off. I could say more. I could
say that one time I passed close he reached a dry hand
around the back of my neck, pulled me to him,
leaned down and laid his silent head on my chest.
Let's say we're writing this together. Let's say I turn
to you now with a question about the wife, how her feet
—slipperless—darkened, on the morning grass, how she
came back years later in a cab to search the house
and did not know her own name. The clock is moving
its hands across the face of heaven. Aunt Yetta stops
between one breath and another. I gather her clothes
into a bundle smelling of talcum and cigarette smoke,
and place it at the foot of her bed. I did that then,
I would do it now, I would do it again tomorrow
if heaven would only look. I would lower the shades
to let the room blossom in darkness, to let Yetta
sleep on long past noon and even into the darkness
of the next day and the next and the next
while a name hangs in the brilliant morning air.

MY BROTHER ABEL, THE WOUNDED

He drew our future in the dirt
with a broken knife he kept
hidden in a green wine bottle
under the sycamore. A circle meant
a perfect year in the absolute.
A straight line signified, but what
he wouldn't say, laughing when
I asked and repeating, "Better not
to know more than you need
to know." Soon I'd be sixteen,
small for my age but not scared,
perhaps because he drew me toward
a large X he called our manhood.
"Right there," he'd say, "you and I
will give no quarter and ask for none."
That was the March I planted roses
beside the back fence, and it snowed
almost into summer, the year
I found African daisies and stole
them from a neighbor's yard
to plant in mine. Later when the war
darkened the headlines, and I
collected beer bottles in the alley
to trade for turnip seeds and put
in rhubarb and prayed the cold
held off, I'd waken in the dark
to see him hunched by the radio
at all hours. In the morning
I'd find black flags inked across
the northern coast of Africa,
black for them, black for us,
until one day the map was gone,
and he took to late night walks
even in the heavy rains of autumn
while the windows smeared my face
before me, while the roof drummed

the steady rhythm of our blood
until I fell into a dreamless
winter sleep he never wakened from.

EDWARD LIEBERMAN, ENTREPRENEUR, FOUR YEARS AFTER THE BURNINGS ON OKINAWA

The light sifts down from the naked bulb
he's quickened with a string. He speaks
to no one out of the well of his anger.
He says, "I hate this," and he stops.
He means more than this one-man shop
on Grand River where he stores the drive-
shafts, bearings, and U-joints swiped
from the Rockwell Arsenal. He means
the stalled traffic outside, the semis
barking and coughing, the gray floor
inside littered with crowded pallets
so filthy they seem furred. He means
the single desk and chair, the hat rack
holding no hats, he even means the phone
he's become so good at, for he's learned
to give nothing away that matters and still
sound serious, to say, "No, we never
allow that much time," and, "Pretty good,
and you?" in a voice so deep even he
doesn't know it. Wardie, everyone's cousin,
still in his twenties, though the blue-
black double-breasted size forty-six he strains
against makes him look forty, the hard fat
of neck, upper chest, and shoulders draws
him down into the chair, and he swivels
abruptly toward those he can't see. Go ahead,
reach out and stroke the dark stubble,
run a lone cautious finger down the channels
for the tears he spills only in sleep.
He won't bite you. He's Wardie, the lost
brother no one remembers, so give him
the love he can't give himself. Feel him
shudder and draw back, not because he kept
his word and killed, not because your thought
became his act, but because it came to this.

LISTEN CAREFULLY

My sister rises from our bed hours before dawn.
I smell her first cigarette and fall back asleep
until she sits on the foot of the bed to pull
on her boots. I shouldn't look, but I do,
knowing she's still naked from the waist up.
She sees me looking and smiles, musses my hair,
whispers something secret into my ear, something
I can't tell anyone because it makes no sense.
Hours later I waken in an empty room
smelling of no yesterdays. The sunlight streams
across the foot of the bed, and for a moment
I actually think it's Saturday, and I'm free.
Let me be frank about this: my older sister
is not smart. I answer all her mail for her,
and on Sundays I even make dinner because
the one cookbook confuses her, although
it claims to be the way to a man's heart.
She wants to learn the way, she wants
a husband, she tells me, but at twenty-six she's
beginning to wonder. She makes good money
doing piece work, assembling the cups that cap
the four ends of a cross of a universal joint.
I've seen her at work, her face cut with slashes
of grease while with tweezers she positions
the tiny rods faster than you or I could ever,
her eyes fixed behind goggles, her mind God
knows where, roaming over all the errors
she thinks make her life. She doesn't know why
her men aren't good to her. I've rubbed
hand cream into the bruises on her shoulders,
I've seen what they've done, I've even cried
along with her. By now I believe I know
exactly what you're thinking. Although I don't
get home until after one, we sleep
in the same bed every night, unless she's
not home. If you're thinking there's no way
we wouldn't be driven to each other, no way

we could resist, no way someone as wronged
as my beautiful sister could have a choice
about something so basic, then you're
the one who's wrong. You haven't heard a word.

THE SPANISH LESSON

In an overstuffed chair, Trotsky sits half asleep.
 Sr. Ruiz paces the floor,
hands clasped behind his back like the old men
 of my boyhood. He could be
one of the old men of my boyhood, his cigar
 unlit and reduced to a damp stub,
his gray curls jutting out from his fine Mayan skull.

Before the lesson ends Sr. Ruiz will demand to know
 Sr. Trotsky's theory of battle,
he will ask if the writings of Clausewitz
 played a role in the triumph
of the forces of light over darkness, in the use
 of cavalry in the last stages
of a war like no other, the first great new war.

Quietly Trotsky will sigh. He too could be one
 of the old men of my boyhood
with a glass of yellow tea cooling on the arm
 of his chair, with his glasses
sliding down his hooked nose, his reddened eyes
 closed against the intrusion
of questions no longer worth answering, no

longer of interest to a man who wants to know
 the words for a wool suit,
the proper method of ordering a five-course meal
 that will not corrupt
his stomach or inflame a liver already damaged.
 Let me make Sr. Trotsky
one of the serious old men of my boyhood,

let me change his name to Josef Prisckulnick
    who crossed from Scotland in '05
on the good ship *Arcadia* and spent two months
    on Ellis Island because a passenger
came down with smallpox two days out of Glasgow
    and died, unmourned, in transit.
Thus will I change the history of the world.

It is so easy to change the history of the world;
    all you have to do is make Leon Trotsky
my dear grandfather in the city of Detroit, a vendor
    instead of a victim. Let him
remain Jewish, let him wear glasses, let him drink
    cold tea through his false teeth,
let the dead rise, let Sr. Ruiz question the wind.

MY MOTHER WITH PURSE THE SUMMER THEY MURDERED THE SPANISH POET

Had she looked out the window she would have seen a quiet street,
each house with a single maple or elm browning in the sun
at the end of summer, the black Fords and Plymouths gleaming
in their fresh wax, the neighbor children returning home
dark suited or white frocked from their Christian studies.

Had she looked out she would have seen the world she crossed
the world to find. Instead she unclasps the leather purse
to make sure she has everything: mirror, lipstick, billfold,
her cards of identity, her checkbook with the week's balance
correctly entered, two monogramed, embroidered handkerchiefs

to blot and hold the tears, for—dark veiled—she's on her way
to meet her husband, gone three years now into the sour earth
of Michigan. Can the long white root a man in time becomes
talk back to one who chose to stay on the far shore
of his departure? Before the day ends, she'll find out.

She will hunch over tea leaves, she will open her palms,
first the hardened hand of the wage earner, then the soft one
that opens to the heart. To see, she will close her eyes;
to hear, she will stop her ears, and the words will be
wrong or no words at all, teeth striking teeth, the tongue

doubled back upon itself, the blackened lips vanished
into the hole of the throat. But for now she looks up.
It is summer, 1936. The first hints of autumn
mist on a row of curtained windows that look in on us
as my mother, perfumed, leans down to brush my mouth with hers,

once, to say my name, precisely, in English. Later
two women will pretend they have reached two other worlds,
the one behind and the one ahead. As they keen
in the darkness perhaps only one will pretend, perhaps
neither, for who shall question that we most clearly see

where no eye is? Wide-eyed he sees nothing. White shirt
worn open, dark trousers with no belt, the olive skin appalled.
When the same wind he loved and sang to touches his cheek
he tries to rub it away. There are others, too, walking over
the flat, gray stones to where a line of men smokes and waits.

The trees have stilled. Had she looked out the window
my mother would have seen each house with its elm or maple
burning, the children drowning in the end of summer, the mist
blurring the eyes of our front windows, the shale hills
above Granada where all time stopped. Her purse snaps shut.

MY FATHER WITH CIGARETTE
TWELVE YEARS BEFORE THE NAZIS
COULD BREAK HIS HEART

I remember the room in which he held
a kitchen match and with his thumbnail
commanded it to flame: a brown sofa,
two easy chairs, one covered with flowers,
a black piano no one ever played half
covered by a long-fringed ornamental scarf
Ray Estrada brought back from Mexico
in 1931. How new the world is, you say.
In that room someone is speaking about money,
asking why it matters, and my father exhales
the blue smoke, and says a million dollars
even in large bills would be impossible.
He's telling me because, I see now, I'm
the one who asked, for I dream of money,
always coins and bills that run through my hands,
money I find in the corners of unknown rooms
or in metal boxes I dig up in the backyard
flower beds of houses I've never seen.
My father rises now and goes to the closet.
It's as though someone were directing a play
and my father's part called for him to stand
so that the audience, which must be you,
could see him in white shirt, dark trousers,
held up by suspenders, a sign of the times,
and conclude he is taller than his son
will ever be, and as he dips into his jacket,
you'll know his role calls for him to exit
by the front door, leaving something
unfinished, the closet light still on,
the cigarette still burning dangerously,
a Yiddish paper folded to the right place
so that a photograph of Hindenburg
in full military regalia swims up
to you out of all the details we lived.
I remember the way the match flared

blue and yellow in the deepening light
of a cool afternoon in early September,
and the sound, part iron, part animal,
part music, as the air rushed toward it
out of my mouth, and his intake of breath
through the Lucky Strike, and the smoke
hanging on after the door closed and the play
ran out of acts and actors, and the audience—
which must be you—grew tired of these lives
that finally come to nothing or no more
than the furniture and the cotton drapes
left open so the darkening sky can seem
to have the last word, with half a moon
and a showering of fake stars to say what
the stars always say about the ordinary.
Oh, you're still here, 60 years later,
you wonder what became of us, why
someone put it in a book, and left
the book open to a page no one reads.
Everything tells you he never came back,
though he did before he didn't, everything
suggests it was the year Hitler came
to power, the year my grandmother learned
to read English novels and fell in love
with *David Copperfield* and *Oliver Twist*
which she read to me seated on a stool
beside my bed until I fell asleep.
Everything tells you this is a preface
to something important, the Second World War,
the news that leaked back from Poland
that the villages were gone. The truth is—
if there is a truth—I remember the room,
I remember the flame, the blue smoke,
how bright and slippery were the secret coins,
how David Copperfield doubted his own name,
how sweet the stars seemed, peeping and blinking,
how close the moon, how utterly silent the piano.

NOTES

Page 13
Some of the images in "Ask for Nothing" were adapted from Antonio Machado's poem "Fields of Soria."

Page 20
I owe the word "Magpiety" to Czesław Miłosz. See his poem of the same name.

Page 49
The poet referred to in "Winter Words, Manhattan" is Thomas Hardy, whose final book of verse, *Winter Words*, was published posthumously.

Page 57
The title of the poem "My Brother Abel, the Wounded" is an adaptation of the opening of the poem "Abel" by Demetrios Capetanakis, a Greek poet who wrote in English.

Page 64
The man who appears in the penultimate stanza of "My Mother with Purse the Summer They Murdered the Spanish Poet" is García Lorca, who was assassinated in August of 1936.

Page 66
The poem "My Father with Cigarette Twelve Years Before the Nazis Could Break His Heart" takes place in 1933. It was inspired by a work of the American painter Harry Lieberman.

A NOTE ABOUT THE AUTHOR

Philip Levine was born in 1928 in Detroit and was formally educated there, at the public schools and at Wayne University (now Wayne State University). After a succession of industrial jobs he left the city for good and lived in various parts of the country before settling in Fresno, California, where he taught at the University until his retirement. He has received many awards for his books of poems, most recently the National Book Award in 1991 for *What Work Is*, and the Pulitzer Prize in 1995 for *The Simple Truth*.